AF584435

World Heritage Sites in Australia

Great Barrier Reef, Fraser Island, Royal Exhibition Building and more...

Queensland, South Australia and Victoria

Ellen Millen

First published 2017 by
Redback Publishing
PO Box 357 Frenchs Forest NSW 2086
Australia

978-1-925630-13-8

Author: Ellen Millen
Editor: Jane Hinchey
Designer: Redback Publishing

Original illustrations © Redback Publishing 2017
Originated by Redback Publishing

Printed and bound in China by Leo Paper

Acknowledgements
Abbreviations: l—left, r—right, b—bottom, t—top, c—centre, m—middle
We would like to thank the following for permission to reproduce photographs: (Images © shutterstock) p5b Hung Chung Chih, p28, Sean Heatley

Contents

What Makes a Place Special?

All around the world, people show that they value special places in different ways. Sites that are special because of their history, beauty or spiritual significance are preserved so that they do not deteriorate and will still exist for future generations to enjoy. Special places can be important for just one person, a group or community, or for everyone in the world.

Various groups in communities look after their special places in different ways

UNESCO

UNESCO identifies World Heritage places around the world.

Governments

Governments at all three levels in Australia make laws and regulations to identify, preserve and protect special places.

Community Groups

People in a local area often join together in groups to protect special places from destruction. Protest groups in Australia have been successful in the past in helping to preserve places of natural and built heritage. Many people donate their time and skills to help maintain special places such as bushland sites or historic buildings.

Individuals

Individuals who care about special places can look after them by being careful not to do anything that might degrade a site. Avoiding littering, not lighting campfires in the bush on days of high fire danger, and not engaging in graffiti or other unlawful activities all help to preserve special places.

Special Places

Make your own list of special places. The list could include homes, shops, parks or even a room or a special spot underneath a tree.

- Why are these places special to you?
- Will they still be important to you in the future?
- Are your special places important to anyone else?

Think about the places that are important just for you. Are they the same places that your friends or family think are special? What makes a place special to you?

World Heritage Sites and UNESCO

UNESCO is a division of the United Nations. It assesses sites around the world for their cultural and natural value to humanity. In 2017, there were 1,052 World Heritage Sites worldwide. Nineteen of these are in Australia.

> *"To be included on the World Heritage List, sites must be of outstanding universal value and meet at least one out of ten selection criteria"*

World Heritage Convention

The work on cataloguing World Heritage Sites began in 1972 as a result of an international treaty known as the World Heritage Convention. Australia was one of the first nations to become involved. Once a World Heritage Site has been determined, the country in which it exists must preserve and protect that site. Countries which have signed the treaty can work together to preserve sites that are of international importance.

World Heritage Committee

The World Heritage Committee is a group of some of the member countries of the United Nations. Committee members serve a fixed term. The role of this committee is to administer all matters relating to World Heritage Sites listings. Australia has been a committee member on a number of occasions.

UNESCO's World Heritage Mission

- To encourage more countries to sign the World Heritage Convention and contribute sites.
- To encourage countries to set up management plans for their sites.
- To provide emergency and technical assistance.
- To encourage local populations to become involved in preserving sites.

Threats to UNESCO World Heritage Sites

World Heritage Sites that are in danger of destruction are listed by UNESCO in their List of World Heritage in Danger. None of the sites in Australia are currently on this list. This is due to the diligent work undertaken by governments and individuals in Australia, and the high regard that Australians have for their heritage sites.

Threats to sites on the List of World Heritage in Danger currently include:

- Natural disasters like earthquakes or cyclones
- Wars and civil conflict
- Uncontrolled expansion of towns and cities
- Unchecked tourist development
- Neglect
- Lack of funds
- Pollution
- Poaching

In 2017, there were 55 sites listed by UNESCO as being under threat.

Hieropolis-Pamukkale, Turkey

Site of Troy, Turkey

World Heritage Fund

Member nations contribute to the World Heritage Fund. Countries that do not have the financial resources to care for a site can apply for funding to assist them.

Chitwan National Park, Nepal

Saving World Heritage Sites

UNESCO has been involved in saving some of the world's most iconic sites and their surroundings, including:

- Angkor, Cambodia
- Dubrovnik, Croatia
- Giza Pyramids, Egypt
- Delphi, Greece
- Abu Simbel, Egypt
- Venice, Italy

Fortified City of Carcassone, France

What is a Plan of Action?

Before setting out to protect a heritage site, it is important to have a Plan of Action. This plan will help to make the conservation process efficient and therefore more effective. Whether the heritage site or special place is being cared for by a government, a community group or an individual, their Plan of Action can include the following points:

- Set a definite goal.
- List the things that may stop this goal being achieved. Examples are a lack of funds, unfavourable weather or groups which oppose the goal.
- List all the activities that will be required to achieve the goal.
- Set priorities for which activities are the most important.
- Decide who will do the work required to achieve the goal.
- How will the goal affect other people who are not involved?
- Where will the funding come from?
- Work out a timetable for achieving the goal.
- Have regular reviews of the Plan of Action and make changes to it if necessary.

How a Heritage Listing Affects Communities

When a place receives a heritage listing, either from UNESCO, a government body or a private organisation, the listing can result in both positive and negative impacts on the community.

Positive Effects

- The heritage site is preserved for future generations.
- Owners of heritage listed buildings can apply for grants to help maintain them.
- Nations can apply for funding from UNESCO to care for their World Heritage Sites.
- More people know that the site exists.
- The world community can encourage nations to continue preserving their sites.
- Heritage sites produce a positive economic effect through their impact on tourism.

Negative Effects

- Indigenous people living in the area may be stopped from using it as a food source and as a place to perform traditional ceremonies.
- People may be stopped from using land as a holiday campsite.
- People cannot usually take pets with them into natural heritage areas.
- Farmers who have been grazing livestock in an area may be stopped from doing this.
- Houses that receive a heritage listing cannot be demolished or changed. Owners need special permits for any work on their building.
- Access to some areas in natural heritage sites may be restricted.
- The construction of roads and buildings is either not allowed or restricted.

Sustainable Tourism in World Heritage Sites

Tourism is a significant activity in World Heritage Sites. UNESCO advises countries with World Heritage Sites on sustainable ways to manage tourism.

At Australian World Heritage Sites, sustainable management of tourism includes:

- Building boardwalks or raised viewing platforms in natural areas so that tourists do not damage the environment when walking through it
- Closing sites, allowing them to regenerate
- Controlling the provision of sewerage and garbage services
- Restricting or forbidding access to sensitive areas
- Banning pets
- Educating the public on the value of the sites and how to behave when visiting them

Sustainability and World Heritage Sites

- Natural sites are involved in carbon storage in the form of trees and plants.
- Natural sites contribute to the water cycle and to climate regulation.
- Natural sites contribute to maintaining the Earth's biodiversity. This is important for the health of humanity, since many of our new medicines come from research undertaken into the properties of rare plants.
- UNESCO reports that climate change is likely to affect World Heritage Sites.

Q&A

Q. Can a place ever stop being a World Heritage Site?

A. Yes. The Arabian Oryx Sanctuary in Oman and the Elbe Valley in Dresden are no longer listed after failing to meet the requirements for preservation of the sites.

Stonehenge

Heritage Organisations in Australia

The Role of Governments and Heritage Councils

UNESCO is not the only organisation that determines whether places have heritage significance. The three levels of government in Australia, federal, state and local, also compile their own listings of important places. There are many more sites and items on these lists than on the World Heritage List for Australian places. Each state and territory has a Heritage Council which advises government on matters relating to heritage places.

Historic Shipwrecks Program

Shipwrecks more than 75 years old are protected by legislation. No items can be taken from them and divers must not move any part of the ship. Severe penalties apply. Shipwrecks that contain the remains of people, unexploded ammunition on warships or other sensitive contents may have access to them restricted. Anyone who discovers an historic shipwreck must report it to the government department responsible for shipwrecks in the relevant state.

Famous Australian Shipwrecks

- HMS Sirius in Slaughter Bay, Norfolk Island is one of the ships of the First Fleet
- Japanese midget submarine M24 from the Second World War is in the sea off Sydney

Overseas Special Places For Australia Listing

This listing is created by the Australian government.

- ANZAC Cove, Gallipoli
- Kokoda Track, Papua New Guinea
- Howard Florey's Laboratory, Sir William Dunn School of Pathology, UK

National Trust

The National Trust has organisations in each state and territory. Their aim is to preserve and promote Australia's cultural heritage. The National Trusts own over 300 heritage places.

Australian Institute of Architects

The Australian Institute of Architects keeps a list of notable buildings of cultural heritage across Australia. A building's importance is based on its aesthetic, historic, social, spiritual or technical value to the community.

Heritage Homework

Some school buildings around Australia are listed on state heritage registers. Is your school one of them? Are there any heritage listed school buildings in your area?

Shipwreck

ANZAC Cove

Australia's 19 World Heritage Properties (2017)

1. Australian Convict Sites
2. Australian Fossil Mammal Sites (Riversleigh / Naracoorte)
3. Fraser Island
4. Gondwana Rainforests of Australia
5. Great Barrier Reef
6. Greater Blue Mountains Area
7. Heard and McDonald Islands
8. Kakadu National Park
9. Lord Howe Island Group
10. Macquarie Island
11. Ningaloo Coast
12. Purnululu National Park
13. Royal Exhibition Building and Carlton Gardens
14. Shark Bay, Western Australia
15. Sydney Opera House
16. Tasmanian Wilderness
17. Uluru-Kata Tjuta National Park
18. Wet Tropics of Queensland
19. Willandra Lakes Region

Lord Howe Island

All World Heritage Sites in Australia are protected by law under the Environment Protection and Biodiversity Conservation Act 1999.

Cockatoo Island

Old Great North Road

Shark Bay, Western Australia

QUEENSLAND

Great Barrier Reef, QLD

A World Heritage Site since 1981, this magnificent coral reef extends along a large part of Queensland's coast. Besides corals, the reef also provides habitats for an immense range of other marine animals and plants. Made up of 2,500 reefs and islands, the Great Barrier Reef has a unique biodiversity. The islands range from small, sandy islets to the large Whitsunday Islands. These islands provide refuge for migrating animals of all types, including birds, turtles, whales and butterflies.

Prehistory

The Great Barrier Reef may be up to 20 million years old. Our Earth is currently in an interglacial era, which means that sea levels are higher than they have been in the ancient past. During glacial eras, when water was stored as ice at the Poles, large parts of the reef became dry land and the coast of Queensland extended much further to the east.

FAST FACT

The Great Barrier Reef is 2,300 km long and can be seen from space. It is the largest living structure on earth.

Aboriginal History

Aboriginal nations lived along the coast beside the Great Barrier Reef and travelled between its islands. They fished the waters, hunted turtles and gathered shellfish. There have been many archaeological finds along the coast, including evidence of the lifestyle of the Darumbal people who lived around the Rockhampton area. They left shell middens, stone arrangements and scarred trees. Bark from these trees was used to build canoes.

The Aboriginal and Torres Strait Islander custodians continue to use the Great Barrier Reef as a food source and a location for practice of culture.

James Cook

James Cook's ship, the Endeavour, was damaged on the reef in 1770. He mapped the area and found Cook's Passage, which is one of the few safe passages between the open sea and the mainland.

EXPLORE IT YOURSELF

Use Google Maps to find the Great Barrier Reef. Can you locate these islands?

- Green Island
- Heron Island
- Lady Musgrave Island
- Dunk Island
- Hamilton Island

Great Barrier Reef Marine Park

In 1975, the Great Barrier Reef Marine Park was formed. It has different types of environmental protection in various zones. The five major zones are:

- General Use
- Habitat Protection
- Conservation Park
- Marine National Park
- Preservation

Permitted activities in the zones range from limited boating and fishing in the General Use Zone to entry by permit for research only in the Preservation Zone. Large ships must use special shipping lanes.

Threats to the Great Barrier Reef

Crown Of Thorns Starfish

This pest starfish destroys the coral by eating it. There are a number of programs underway to control the Crown of Thorns without introducing dangerous chemicals that would also kill other marine animals.

Development

Ports, tourist sites and towns along the coast have buildings and pollutants that can affect the reef by destroying natural coastal ecosystems.

Shipping

Ships in the reef waters can be a source of pollutants such as oil, waste water and rubbish. Ships need to travel within the reef waters to reach ports along the coast, but they can pose a threat if an accident causes them to release oil into the water.

Climate Change

Coral bleaching results in the death of coral. A rise in the water temperature due to climate change can cause this. In 2016, the reef suffered its most severe bleaching on record.

Tourism

Tourists need accommodation and like to explore the reef and see its wildlife. These activities can place stress on the reef and its water quality.

Agriculture

Run-off from agricultural land on the mainland enters rivers and then ends up on the reef. This water often carries pesticides and fertilisers which damage the marine ecosystems.

Litter Control

Litter can be deposited in the reef by rivers and from boats. Plastic litter is particularly damaging since it does not degrade.

Extreme Weather

Floods on the mainland send water down rivers and into the reef area. This water reduces the salinity of the reef and it also contains silt and pollutants which can kill coral. Cyclones cause structural damage to the reef.

Crown Of Thorns Starfish

Coral bleaching

Future Sustainability of the Great Barrier Reef

Planning for the future sustainability of the Great Barrier Reef has been investigated in the Reef 2050 Long-Term Sustainability Plan. This plan investigates matters that will affect the reef in the future, including dredging, water quality from land runoff, shipping and protection for threatened species.

Gondwana Rainforests of Australia

These sub-tropical rainforests are located in the southeast of Queensland and the northeast of New South Wales. They were first listed as a combined World Heritage site in 1986. Millions of years ago, rainforests such as these covered most of Australia. Some of the plants and trees found in the rainforests are direct descendants of ones that once grew on the ancient continent of Gondwana.

The rainforests are a world repository of very precious vegetation, such as the descendants of ancient ferns, conifers and primitive flowering plants. These plants are only seen as fossils elsewhere in the world.

History of European Settlement in the Gondwana Rainforests

- Early settlers cleared rainforests to provide land for farming and housing.
- Roads and railways were built through the rainforests so that miners and farmers could transport their products to ports and markets in large towns.
- Rainforest trees were logged for their timber.

Threats to the Gondwana Rainforests

- The World Heritage listed areas that form the Gondwana Rainforests are not all connected and some are not very large. This makes their management difficult as the habitat for the plants and animals in the smaller parts is restricted
- Climate change
- Uncontrolled tourism
- Bushfires
- Feral animals

Wet Tropics of Queensland

The Wet Tropics of Queensland extend over 450 kilometres in northeast Australia. They have been a World Heritage Site since 1988. Situated between Townsville and Cooktown, the Wet Tropics are remnants of the tropical rainforests that once covered much larger areas of Queensland than today. The vegetation in these rainforests is biologically important since it includes living examples that are the descendants of nearly every stage of the development of plant life on Earth. Some of these plants are the same as ones that lived on Australia over fifty million years ago, when it was still a part of the ancient continent of Gondwana. The evolution of Australia's unique marsupial animals began in these Gondwanan rainforests. Even Australia's array of eucalypt trees are all probably descended from ancestors which grew in the ancient rainforests, and then gradually evolved to be able to live in drier areas as well. Although it covers only a small portion of Australia, the Wet Tropics site provides a habitat for 40 per cent of all Australia's bird species.

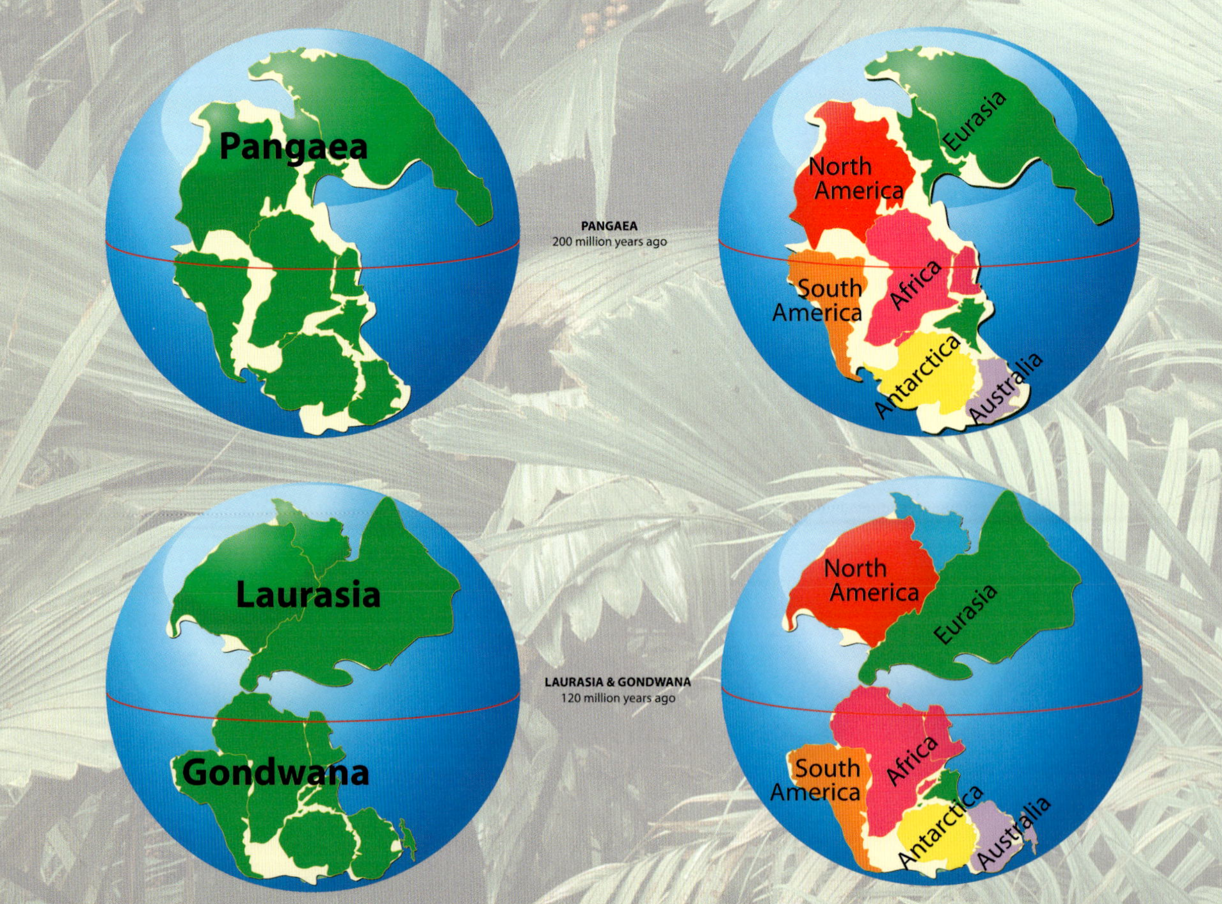

Aboriginal Custodians

There are eighteen Rainforest Aboriginal groups in the Wet Tropics World Heritage Area. Their walking tracks connected all parts of their land, and the course of the Gillies Highway follows one of these routes. The Daintree is the only tropical rainforest in Australia that has an unbroken record of habitation by its Aboriginal custodians.

In 2012, the special techniques developed by the ancestors of the Aboriginal custodians for processing toxic rainforest foods were recognised as developments of national cultural significance. These techniques were described and included as a part of the reason for the national heritage listing of the Wet Tropics of Queensland by the Australian government.

The food technology developed for making toxic plants become edible included:

- Using ovens to soften the foods
- Leaching the toxins out in running water
- Making grooves and pits on grinding tools to collect the toxins

Living according to the demands of the wet and dry seasons, the Rainforest Aboriginal people built sturdy, thatched huts in the drier regions and temporary shelters in the lower areas where flooding occurred. They used controlled burns to ensure their food sources were sustainably managed.

Threats to the Wet Tropics of Queensland

- Climate change
- Extremely high number of species in a relatively small area
- Uncontrolled tourism
- Bushfires
- Feral animals

Daintree National Park, Cape Tribulation

How the Wet Tropics of Queensland are Protected

In 2005, the Wet Tropics World Heritage Area Regional Agreement was created to manage the site. It involves members of the traditional Aboriginal custodians as well as the Australian and Queensland governments. Special groups have been set up to oversee conservation and tourism.

Opposition to the Heritage Listing

Not all members of the community were in favour of the Wet Tropics receiving either a UNESCO or Australian Government heritage listing. People who had lived and worked within the area for many years were worried that their jobs and income would be seriously affected by a heritage listing. The timber industry opposed the heritage listing and demanded compensation for loss of income after logging for timber in the rainforest was made illegal.

Below: Mossman Gorge

Southern Cassowary

The southern cassowary is a large flightless bird that lives in the Wet Tropics rainforests. It is listed as an endangered animal. It requires large areas of rainforest to survive, so the clearing of land by settlers since colonial times has reduced its habitat. Cassowary chicks are eaten by feral dogs and feral pigs destroy cassowary nests and eat the eggs.

Spotted-tailed quoll

Rare animals in the Wet Tropics of QLD

northern bettong
spotted-tailed quoll
yellow-bellied glider
musky rat kangaroo

Fraser Island, QLD

Fraser Island stretches 123 kilometres along the southeast coast of Queensland. It has been on the World Heritage List since 1992.

Heritage Features of Fraser Island

- Largest sand island in the world
- Rare examples of tropical rainforests growing on sand
- Coastal sand dunes
- 250 kilometres of beaches
- Resting site for birds migrating between Siberia and southern Australia
- The Fraser Island dingo is the most pure strain of dingo in eastern Australia

Past Threats to Fraser Island

- Logging of the rainforest has ceased
- Feral animals and weeds are controlled
- Private property on the island is managed well

Current Threats to the Heritage Site

- Bushfires
- Reintroduction of feral animals and weeds
- Impact of tourists
- Use of 4WD vehicles off-road
- Tourists interacting with wild dingoes

Aboriginal History

The Aboriginal name for Fraser Island is K'gari. Archaeological evidence of early occupation includes shell middens, fish traps, scarred trees and the remains of ancient campsites. These finds suggest that Aboriginal people lived on the island at least 5,000 years ago.

FAST FACT
Fraser Island has over 100 freshwater lakes.

Fraser Island's Dingoes

Dingoes are wild animals and can be dangerous. The government has produced these tourist tips on what to do if threatened by a dingo on Fraser Island:

- Never feed dingoes.
- Always stay within arm's reach of children, even small teenagers.
- Walk in groups.
- Do not run. Running or jogging can trigger a negative dingo interaction.
- Camp in fenced areas when possible.
- Lock up food stores and iceboxes (even on a boat).
- Never store food or food containers in tents.
- Secure all rubbish, fish and bait.

Australian Fossil Mammal Site Riversleigh, QLD

The fossil sites at Riversleigh have been on the World Heritage List since 1994. Riversleigh is in the Boodjamulla (Lawn Hill) National Park, near Mount Isa. It has the richest known fossil mammal deposit in Australia. Searches there have revealed fossils from the ancient Gondwanan continent. The site is very remote, and some areas have restricted access.

- Riversleigh is one of the world's ten most important fossil sites.
- Fossils date from 10 million to 30 million years ago.
- The fossils span the change from rainforest to dry woodland and show that most of Australia's unique animals evolved from rainforest ancestors.
- The fossilised remains of a meat-eating kangaroo have been found at Riversleigh.

Management of the Heritage Site

- Grazing of livestock and mining on the heritage site have ceased.
- The Waanyi Advisory Committee provides advice on Indigenous issues at Riversleigh.
- At the Riversleigh Fossil Centre, visitors can see displays showing what the fossil animals would have looked like millions of years ago.

SOUTH AUSTRALIA

Australian Fossil Mammal Site Naracoorte, SA

The fossil sites at Naracoorte have been on the World Heritage List since 1994. At the Wonambi Fossil Centre, visitors can look at scenes that have been created to show the animals and how they would have looked in their ancient environments.

- The fossil caves of Naracoorte are amongst the world's ten most important fossil sites.
- Vertebrate fossils from 530,000 years ago have been found in the caves.
- The caves contain the fossilised remains of animals that were in Australia when humans first arrived 60,000 years ago.
- One of the fossils found is of a marsupial lion. Other fossils are of Ice-Age megafauna.

Protection of the site

Special rules apply to the recording of fossil locations and to fossil removal by palaeontologists. Although mining was allowed in one cave in the 1800s, the caves are now protected and nothing can be taken out of them without permission.

Tourism

Some of the Naracoorte caves have been opened to the public and altered to provide easy access. A tour of the Victoria Fossil Cave allows visitors to see the places where fossil skeletons are still being found.

Inside the caves at The Naracoorte Caves National Park

Skeleton of a Marsupial Lion

Royal Exhibition Building and Carlton Gardens, VIC

Built for the 1880 Melbourne International Exhibition, this heritage property is one of the last exhibition style buildings from the era still left in the world. It was World Heritage listed in 2004. The historic layout and fountains of the surrounding Carlton Gardens have been listed for preservation as well. The style of the building, with a large dome, towers and many windows is similar to the design of exhibition buildings in other countries, most of which are no longer standing. The influence of European palace architecture and garden design is obvious.

During the mid 1800s to the early 1900s, exhibitions showing industrial and technological progress were popular around the world. The event held in Melbourne helped to bring Australia and its products to the notice of markets overseas.

The site has an added importance, as it was the place where the first Australian Parliament sat in 1901, before Canberra became the nation's capital.

Safety Versus History

It is not always possible to restore a heritage building to exactly the way it was in the past. Modern safety features need to be considered, particularly since the Royal Exhibition Building is still used for events open to the public. Because of this, the original timber staircases, which were a fire risk, have been replaced with cement stairs instead.

Did You Know?

A similar Garden Palace in Sydney burned down in 1882. Its dome made it the tallest building in Sydney at the time.

Glossary

aesthetic	relating to beauty
dredging	clearing a waterway of mud or sand
heritage	thing or characteristic that is handed down from previous generations
islet	tiny island
megafauna	giant animals now only seen as fossils
palaeontologist	fossil researcher
prehistory	time before history was recorded by humans
shell middens	places where the debris from eating shellfish and other food has accumulated over time
species	separate group of animals or plants
vertebrate	having a backbone
UNESCO	United Nations Educational, Scientific and Cultural Organization

Index

Visit these websites to find out more about Australia's World Heritage Sites and special places

whc.unesco.org/en/list
www.environment.gov.au/heritage